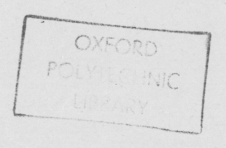

For Nancy

British Library Cataloguing
in Publication Data
Roger was a razor fish.
1. Children's poetry
I. Bennett, Jill II. Roffey, Maureen
821'.9'1408   P N6110.C4
I S B N 0–370–30352–0

This selection © Jill Bennett 1980
Illustrations © Maureen Roffey 1980
Printed and bound in Great Britain for
The Bodley Head Ltd
9 Bow Street, London W C 2 E 7 A L
by William Clowes (Beccles) Limited
First published 1980

Roger was a Razor Fish

and other poems

compiled by **JILL BENNETT**

illustrated by **MAUREEN ROFFEY**

THE BODLEY HEAD
LONDON SYDNEY
TORONTO

ICE

When it is the winter time
I run up the street
And I make the ice laugh
With my little feet—
'Crickle, crackle, crickle
Crrreeet, crrreeet, crrreeet.'

Dorothy Aldi

AMPLIGHTER BARN

I can play
in the prickly hay
and I can find
where the chickens lay
and take off my shoes
and stay
and stay
in the tickly hay
on a rainy day.

Myra Cohn Livingston

MY NAME IS...

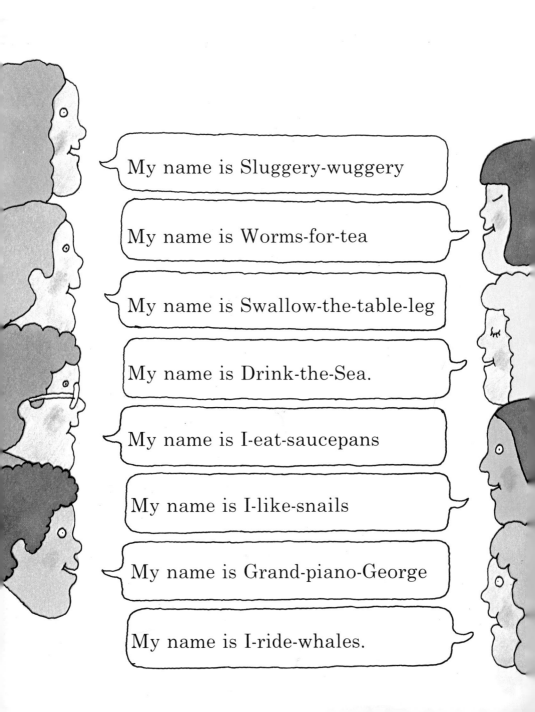

My name is Sluggery-wuggery

My name is Worms-for-tea

My name is Swallow-the-table-leg

My name is Drink-the-Sea.

My name is I-eat-saucepans

My name is I-like-snails

My name is Grand-piano-George

My name is I-ride-whales.

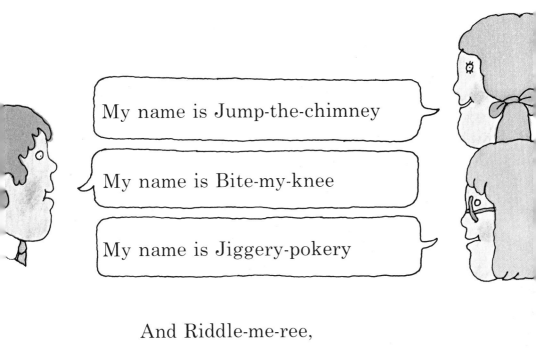

My name is Jump-the-chimney

My name is Bite-my-knee

My name is Jiggery-pokery

And Riddle-me-ree,

and M E.

Pauline Clarke

FIRE

Anon.

BUILDINGS

Buildings are a great surprise,
Every one's a different size.

Offices
grow
long
and
high,
tall
enough
to
touch
the
sky.

Houses seem
more like a box,
made of glue
and building blocks.

Every time you look, you see
Buildings shaped quite differently.

Myra Cohn Livingston

WHAT SOMEONE SAID
WHEN HE WAS SPANKED
ON THE DAY BEFORE HIS BIRTHDA

Some day
I may
Pack my bag and run away.
Some day
I may.
– But not today.

Some night
I might
Slip away in the moonlight.
I might.
Some night.
– But not tonight.

Some night.
Some day.
I might.
I may.
– But right now I think I'll stay.

John Ciardi

SNAIL

Snail upon the wall,
Have you got at all
Anything to tell
About your shell?

Only this, my child –
When the wind is wild,
Or when the sun is hot,
It's all I've got.

John Drinkwat

THE TICKLE RHYME

'Who's that tickling my back?' said the wall.
'Me,' said a small
Caterpillar. 'I'm learning
To crawl.'

Ian Serraillier

ROGER WAS A RAZOR FISH

Roger was a razor fish
as sharp as he could be.
He said to Calvin Catfish,

'I'll shave you
for a fee.'

'No thanks,'
said Calvin Catfish,
'I like me like I be.'
And with his whiskers
on his face
he headed out to sea.

Al Pittman

'QUACK!' SAID THE BILLY-GOAT

'QUACK!'

said the billy-goat

'OINK!'

said the hen.

'MIAOW!'

said the little chick
Running in the pen.

'HOBBLE-GOBBLE!'

said the dog.

'HEE-HAW!'

the turkey cried.

The duck began to moo.

All at once the sheep went,

'COCK-A-DOODLE-DOO!'

The owl coughed
   and cleared his throat
And he began to bleat.

'BOW-WOW!'

said the cock
Swimming in the leat.

'CHEEP-CHEEP!'

said the cat
As she began to fly.

FARMER'S BEEN
AND LAID AN EGG –
THAT'S THE REASON WHY.'

Charles Causley

TREE HOUSE

A tree house, a free house,
A secret you and me house,
A high up in the leafy branches
Cozy as can be house.

A street house, a neat house,
Be sure and wipe your feet house
Is not my kind of house at all—

Let's go live
in a tree house.

Shel Silverstein

LITTLE MISS TUCKETT

Little Miss Tuckett
Sat on a bucket,
Eating some peaches and cream.
There came a grasshopper
And tried hard to stop her,
But she said, 'Go away, or I'll scream.'

An

GER

I'm a tiger
Striped with fur
Don't come near
Or I might Grrr
Don't come near
Or I might growl
Don't come near
Or I might
BITE!

Mary Ann Hoberman

SIX LITTLE MICE

Six little mice sat down to spin;

Pussy passed by and she peeped in.
What are you doing, my little men?

Weaving coats for gentlemen.

Shall I come in and cut off your threads?
No, no, Mistress Pussy, you'd bite off our heads.

Oh, no, I'll not; I'll help you to spin.
That may be so, but you don't come in.

Anon.

VE LITTLE OWLS

Five little owls in an old elm-tree,
Fluffy and puffy as owls could be,
Blinking and winking with big round eyes
At the big round moon that hung in the skies:
As I passed beneath, I could hear one say,
'There'll be mouse for supper, there will, to-day!'
Then all of them hooted 'Tu-whit, Tu-whoo!
Yes, mouse for supper, Hoo hoo, Hoo hoo!'

Anon.

JOHN

John could take his clothes off
but could not put them on.

His patient mother dressed him,

and said to little John,

'Now, John!
    You keep your things on.'

But John had long since gone—
and left a trail of sneakers
and small things in the sun,

so she would know to find him
wherever he might run.

And at the end of every trail
stood Mrs Jones & Son,

she with all his little clothes,
and little John—with none!

For John could take his clothes off
but could not put them on.

His patient mother dressed him

and on went little John—
and on—
    and on—
       and on—

N. M. Bodecker

PUNCH AND JUDY

Punch and Judy
  Fought for a pie;
Punch gave Judy
  A knock in the eye.
Says Punch to Judy,
  Will you have any more?
Says Judy to Punch,
  My eye is too sore.

Anon.

RS PECK-PIGEON

Mrs Peck-Pigeon
Is picking for bread,
Bob—bob—bob
Goes her little round head.
Tame as a pussy-cat
In the street,
Step—step—step
Go her little red feet.
With her little red feet
And her little round head,
Mrs Peck-Pigeon
Goes picking for bread.

Eleanor Farjeon

MY PUPPY

It's funny
my puppy
knows just how I feel.

When I'm happy
he's yappy
and squirms like an eel.

When I'm grumpy
he's slumpy
and stays at my heel.

It's funny
my puppy
knows such a great deal.

Aileen Fisher

WITCH, WITCH

'Witch, witch, where do you fly?' . . .
'Under the clouds and over the sky.'

'Witch, witch, what do you eat?' . . .
'Little black apples from Hurricane Street.'

'Witch, witch, what do you drink?' . . .
'Vinegar, blacking and good red ink.'

'Witch, witch, where do you sleep?' . . .
'Up in the clouds where pillows are cheap.'

Rose Fyleman

THIS IS MY ROCK

This is my rock,
And here I run
To steal the secret of the sun;

This is my rock,
And here come I
Before the night has swept the sky;

This is my rock,
This is the place
I meet the evening face to face.

David McCord

THE PASTURE

I'm going out to clean the pasture spring;
I'll only stop to rake the leaves away
(And wait to watch the water clear, I may):
I sha'n't be gone long. – You come too.

I'm going out to fetch the little calf
That's standing by the mother. It's so young
It totters when she licks it with her tongue.
I sha'n't be gone long. – You come too.

Robert Frost

ACKNOWLEDGEMENTS

Thanks are due to the following for permission to reprint copyright material : 'Ice' reprinted by permission of G.P. Putnam's Sons from *Everything and Anything* by Dorothy Aldis. Copyright ©1925, 26, 27, renewed copyright © 1953, 54, 55 by Dorothy Aldis; 'Lamplighter Barn' from *Wide Awake and Other Poems*,© 1959 by Myra Cohn Livingston. Reprinted by permission of Harcourt Brace Jovanovich, Inc.; Abelard-Schuman Ltd for 'My Name Is ...' by Pauline Clarke from *Silver Bells and Cockle Shells*; 'Buildings' from *Whispers and Other Poems* published by Harcourt, Brace & World, Inc. Copyright © 1958 by Myra Cohn Livingston. Reprinted by permission of McIntosh and Otis, Inc.; 'What Someone Said When He Was Spanked On The Day Before His Birthday' from *You Know Who*, copyright © 1964 by John Ciardi. Reprinted by permission of J. B. Lippincott, Publishers, Inc.; Samuel French Ltd for 'Snail' by John Drinkwater; 'The Tickle Rhyme' from *The Monster Horse* published by Oxford University Press. Copyright ©1950 Ian Serraillier; 'Roger was a Razor Fish' used by permission from Breakwater Books Ltd, Canada's Atlantic Publisher, 277 Duckwater Street, St John's, Newfoundland. Originally appeared in *Down By Jim Long's Stage*. ©1976, Al Pittman; David Higham Associates Limited for 'Quack! said the Billy-Goat' by Charles Causley from *Figgie Hobbin* published by Macmillan, and 'Mrs Peck-Pigeon' by Eleanor Farjeon from *Silver Sand and Snow* published by Michael Joseph; 'Tree House' from *Where the Sidewalk Ends*: the poems and drawings of Shel Silverstein. Copyright © 1974 by Shel Silverstein. Reprinted by permission of Harper & Row, Publishers, Inc.; 'Tiger' from *Hello and Good-by* published by Little, Brown, Inc. Reprinted by permission of Russell & Volkening, Inc. as agents for the Author. Copyright © 1959 by Mary Ann Hoberman; 'John' from *Let's Marry Said the Cherry and Other Nonsense Poems* by N.M. Bodecker (A Margaret K. McElderry Book). Copyright © 1974 by N.M. Bodecker. Used by permission of Atheneum Publishers, New York and Faber and Faber Ltd, London; 'My Puppy' from *Up the Windy Hill* by Aileen Fisher. Reprinted by permission of Scott, Foresman and Company; 'Witch, Witch' from *Fifty-One New Nursery Rhymes* by Rose Fyleman. Copyright ©1931, 1932 by Doubleday & Company, Inc. Reprinted by permission of the publisher in the U.S.A. and The Society of Authors as the literary representative of the Estate of Rose Fyleman; 'This Is My Rock' from *One at a Time* by David McCord, by permission of Little, Brown and Co. Inc. and George G. Harrap & Company Limited, London. Copyright 1929 ©1957 by David McCord; 'The Pasture' from *The Poetry of Robert Frost* edited by Edward Connery Lathem. Copyright 1939, ©1967, 1969 by Holt, Rinehart and Winston. Reprinted by permission of Holt, Rinehart and Winston, Publishers, New York, and Jonathan Cape Limited, London, on behalf of the Estate of Robert Frost.